A STARRY MESSAGE

Two neutron stars collide in this artist's image.

On August 17, 2017, a message arrived from deep space. It began as a low rumble and ended with a sudden *bloop*. The message didn't come from aliens. It came from a collision between two **neutron stars**.

As they crashed together, the neutron stars released enormous amounts of energy. The energy caused **atoms** in the stars to change into elements such as gold and lead. The explosion was so powerful that space rippled as waves of **gravity** rushed away from the blast.

Contents

For science teachers everywhere—thank you

Lerner Publications Company
A division of Lerner Publishing Group, Inc.
241 First Avenue North
Minneapolis, MN 55401 USA

For reading levels and more information, look up this title at www.lernerbooks.com.

Main body text set in Aptifer Sans LT Pro Regular 12/18.
Typeface provided by Linotype AG.

Library of Congress Cataloging-in-Publication Data

Names: Peterson, Christy, author.
Title: Breakthroughs in stars research / Christy Peterson.
Description: Minneapolis : Lerner Publications, [2018] | Series: Space exploration
    (Alternator books) | Audience: Ages 8–12. | Audience: Grades 4 to 6. | Includes
    bibliographical references and index.
Identifiers: LCCN 2018016818 (print) | LCCN 2018025129 (ebook) |
    ISBN 9781541543751 (eb pdf) | ISBN 9781541538719 (lb : alk. paper)
Subjects: LCSH: Astronomy—Research—Juvenile literature. | Stars—Juvenile
    literature.
Classification: LCC QB61 (ebook) | LCC QB61 .P477 2018 (print) | DDC 523.807—dc23

LC record available at https://lccn.loc.gov/2018016818

Manufactured in the United States of America
1-45054-35881-8/7/2018

ALTERNATOR
BOOKS™

BREAKTHROUGHS IN
STARS
RESEARCH

Christy Peterson

Lerner Publications ◆ Minneapolis

By the time they reached Earth, the **gravitational waves** were smaller than an atom. Yet scientists detected them using sensitive new machines. By studying the gravitational waves, scientists learned more about neutron stars. They calculated how big the largest neutron stars could be. Scientists located the direction the waves had come from, allowing people to point telescopes toward the colliding stars. Studying light from the explosion helped scientists prove that neutron star collisions spread gold and other elements around the universe.

Scientists used a computer program to create this simulated image of gravitational waves.

EYES ON THE UNIVERSE

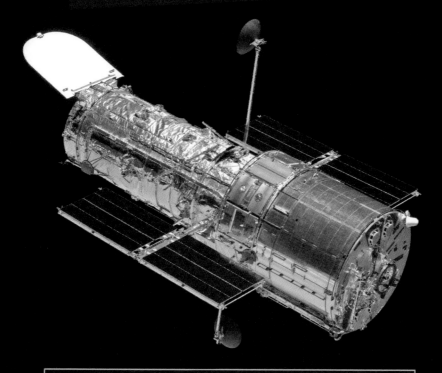

The Hubble Space Telescope is 45.3 feet (13.8 m) long.

Even on the clearest night, our **atmosphere** makes stars look fuzzy. In 1990 the National Aeronautics and Space Administration (NASA) launched the Hubble Space Telescope to solve this problem. From its position in orbit around Earth, Hubble can show stars and other objects in space much more clearly than telescopes on Earth can.

STEM FOCUS

Imagine the ripples, or waves, that form when you drop a rock into a pond. The distance from the top of one wave to the top of the next is a wavelength. Light travels in waves too. Different kinds of light have different wavelengths.

Stars give off light in many wavelengths. Some of this light we can see. Light with other wavelengths, such as X-rays, are invisible to the human eye. Telescopes such as Hubble can detect different wavelengths and allow scientists to study light from stars we can't see with our eyes.

Observing light from stars can tell us a lot. Instruments on Hubble split light into different wavelengths. Since different elements in stars give off different wavelengths of light, studying the light can tell scientists exactly what makes up a star. Light can even reveal if a planet is orbiting a star. Hubble can detect small changes in a star's light as planets pass in front of the star.

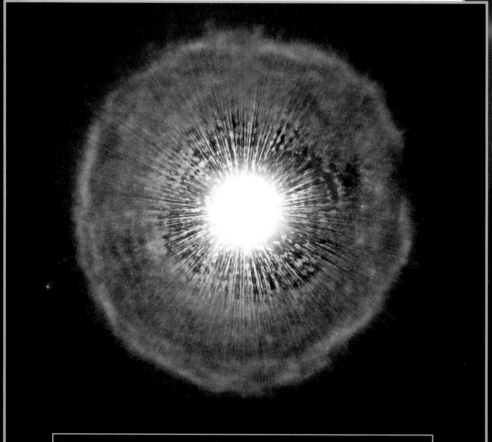

Stars give off light in many wavelengths that humans can't see without the help of scientific instruments.

The Carina Nebula is about 7,500 light-years from Earth. Our sun was likely created in a similar nebula billions of years ago.

THE LIVES OF STARS

A star forms in a nebula, a huge cloud of dust and gases such as hydrogen and helium. Gravity squishes the dust and gas together so tightly that hydrogen atoms in the clouds begin to fuse together. This releases huge amounts of energy. When the force of the released energy matches the force of the gravity pushing in, a star is born. The star is a collection of superheated atoms called **plasma**.

Star creation is hard to observe because dust and gas block the wavelengths of light we can see. But Hubble's instruments can detect wavelengths of light that aren't blocked. This allows scientists to see through the dust clouds and study how new stars form. Hubble's amazing instruments also allow scientists to study stars at other phases of their lives.

This Hubble image shows the Horsehead Nebula. The nebula blocks some of the light from stars.

Some of the biggest stars in the universe are red giants.

A star usually remains stable as long as it has hydrogen atoms to fuse. When the hydrogen runs out, the energy the star gives off weakens. Gravity crushes the star, which causes it to get hotter. The additional heat allows helium atoms to fuse together. When this happens to a medium-size star like our sun, it grows into a much bigger star called a red giant.

When the helium runs low in a red giant, gravity pushes in again. The pressure causes the star to explode. The blast pushes gas and dust into space, creating a nebula. All that remains of the original star is a slowly cooling star called a white dwarf. The cycle will begin again when dust and gas in the nebula form new stars.

An image from Hubble shows a red giant star sending gas and dust into space to form a nebula.

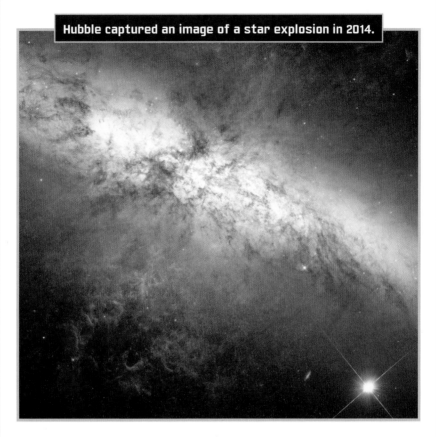

Hubble captured an image of a star explosion in 2014.

Giant stars die much more dramatically. At the end of their lives, they collapse and burst in massive explosions called **supernovas**. The star's remains compress and become either a neutron star or, if the star was massive enough, a **black hole**.

In 1987 Supernova 1987A appeared in the sky. Hubble has taken photographs of this supernova for almost thirty years. These images will help scientists learn more about stellar explosions and predict which stars could become supernovas next.

CHAPTER 2

A STAR FAMILY ALBUM

An artist's image of the Milky Way galaxy

All stars give off heat and light. They are born and die in similar ways. But the Milky Way galaxy is home to more than one hundred billion stars, and none is the same. To understand how stars compare to one another, scientists need to study more stars—a lot more.

On December 19, 2013, a rocket carried the *Gaia* spacecraft into orbit. *Gaia* carries two telescopes and the largest digital camera ever used in space. It also has instruments that analyze light coming from stars. *Gaia*'s mission is to collect data on more than one billion stars in our galaxy.

Gaia's mission is expected to last about five years.

Gaia will send about one million gigabytes of data to Earth during its mission. That's the same amount of data as 250 million songs! Scientists and computer experts—450 in all—work together on the Gaia mission. They organize the data and create tools to make the information easier to use.

Operators at the European Space Agency control the Gaia mission and other space exploration projects.

With billions of stars in the Milky Way, creating a 3D star map is an enormous undertaking.

FROM DATA TO TOOLS

One tool the Gaia mission team created is a detailed 3D map of more than one billion stars in our galaxy. Using this map, scientists can see patterns. They see areas where stars cluster together. They can see where new stars form and where the oldest stars in the galaxy shine. Observing so many stars helps scientists learn how our galaxy got its start.

The team also used data from *Gaia* to create a star catalog. Objects in space move and change position relative to one another. The catalog contains a star's position, speed, and direction compared to Earth. This information reveals where each star came from and where it is headed. Knowing past locations of stars helps scientists understand how our galaxy looked when it was younger. Predicting the future location of stars allows scientists to understand what our galaxy will look like millions of years from now.

Galaxies have different shapes, and *Gaia* will help scientists predict the Milky Way's future shape.

THE STAR IN OUR BACKYARD

Earth has a magnetic field that helps protect the planet from the sun.

Without the sun, life on Earth would not exist. Yet our backyard star is a fierce, violent ball of superheated plasma. A stream of **charged particles** called **solar wind** pours into space from the sun. And the sun's surface sometimes erupts in massive explosions that reach far into the solar system. These events can destroy satellites and disrupt power systems on Earth.

On Earth, weather predictions help keep people and property safe. Scientists want to be able to predict the intensity of solar wind and explosions too. To learn more about the sun, NASA launched the Solar Dynamics Observatory in 2010. The spacecraft takes pictures of the sun in ten wavelengths of light. It also has the Helioseismic and Magnetic Imager. This instrument analyzes plasma moving on the sun's surface, helping scientists understand what's going on inside.

This image from the Solar Dynamics Observatory shows parts of the sun's magnetic fields as white lines swirling near the surface.

STEM FOCUS

In a refrigerator magnet, a magnetic field forms when charged particles called electrons move in the same direction. You can't see a magnetic field, but if you push two magnets together, you can feel it. The sun's plasma consists of charged particles, so the sun creates massive magnetic fields.

Just like with refrigerator magnets, scientists can't see the sun's magnetic fields. They see evidence of them on the sun's surface. **Sunspots** form when magnetic fields bubble up from below. Magnetic fields also create swirling plasma loops.

Lines highlight magnetic fields in this artist's image.

Flares burst out from the sun's surface.

LEARNING WHAT MAKES THE SUN TICK

In July 2017, scientists looking at images from the Solar Dynamics Observatory spotted a cluster of sunspots. These dark areas were caused by strong magnetic fields below the surface. As scientists continued to observe the sunspots, quick bursts of light, or flares, erupted.

Then, on July 14, a huge bubble of plasma called a coronal mass ejection exploded from the spots. Scientists watched the storm's path through space. Two days later, the charged particles hit Earth's magnetic field, causing beautiful **auroras** at the poles and disrupting satellites and power systems.

Auroras often appear in the sky near Earth's poles. They're also called southern lights or northern lights.

Scientists also studied a group of sunspots that did not produce a coronal mass ejection. They wanted to understand what made these spots different. Activity on the sun's surface showed that magnetic fields surrounded the sunspots. Though small flares escaped, scientists think magnetic fields above the sunspots prevented magnetic fields below the sunspots from creating a larger eruption. This discovery may help scientists predict coronal mass ejections. Building a picture of how the sun works inside and out will help scientists protect our planet from the sun's violent outbursts.

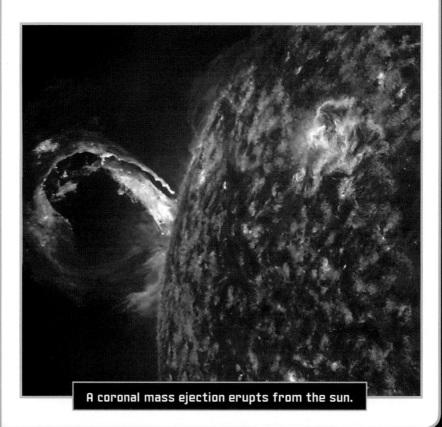

A coronal mass ejection erupts from the sun.

THE NEXT CHAPTER

The European Space Agency is one of several organizations seeking to learn more about gravitational waves.

Scientists want to learn more about stars, and studying gravitational waves can help. Gravitational waves give scientists a picture of objects and events that they can't see in other ways. But Earth isn't a great place to detect these waves. The planet's gravity, earthquakes, and even passing trucks create vibrations that interfere with gravitational wave detectors.

Scientists at the European Space Agency plan to send a gravitational wave detector into space in 2034. The Laser Interferometer Space Antenna will cover a huge area of space in the search for gravitational waves. In space the antenna won't have to deal with the vibrations that interfere with detectors on Earth.

The Laser Interferometer Space Antenna will consist of three spacecraft positioned in a triangle.

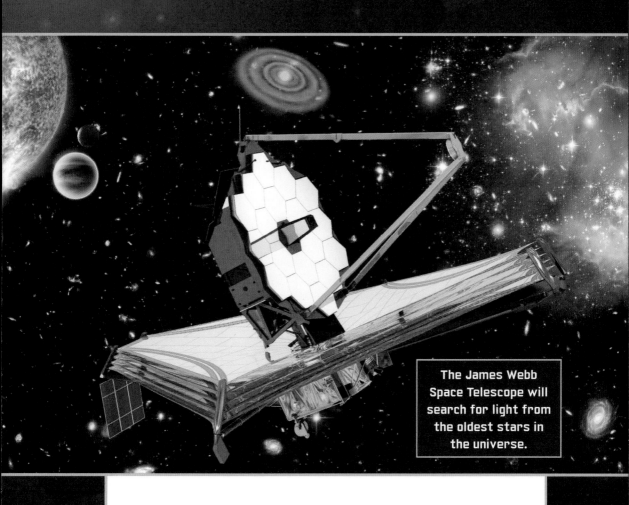

The James Webb Space Telescope will search for light from the oldest stars in the universe.

NEW EYES ON THE UNIVERSE

In 2018 scientists released Hubble images of the most distant stars ever seen. These stars are part of an ancient galaxy that formed over thirteen billion years ago. In the images, the stars clump together in a red smear. In 2021 NASA plans to launch the James Webb Space Telescope. Its powerful instruments should give us an even better view of these stars and the universe.

Scientists have big plans to study our own star too. In 2018 NASA launched the Parker Solar Probe. The probe will fly into the outer part of the sun, giving us the closest view ever of the star. New tools like the solar probe will add to the mountains of data we have already about stars. As scientists make sense of the data, they'll discover new breakthroughs in stars research and new questions to explore.

The Parker Solar Probe is named after Eugene Parker, a University of Chicago physicist who has made important discoveries about how stars give off energy.

•••• WHAT THE TECH? ••••

In 1977 NASA launched *Voyager 1* (*below*) to explore Jupiter and Saturn. It completed its mission and continued soaring through space. Then it helped scientists answer a big question: Where is the edge of the solar system?

The sun's solar wind reaches far beyond the planets. Eventually the solar wind stops and gives way to interstellar space, the areas between stars. The point where solar wind ends is the heliopause. In August 2012, *Voyager 1* became the first spacecraft to pass the heliopause. It sent information about the heliopause to Earth. Then it kept flying into interstellar space, more than 11 billion miles (17.7 billion km) from the sun.

atmosphere: the mix of gases surrounding a planet

atoms: the smallest possible units of an element

auroras: lights in the sky near the north and south poles caused by particles from the sun interacting with Earth's magnetic field

black hole: a region in space with such strong gravity that not even light can escape

charged particles: tiny bits of matter that carry an electrical charge

gravitational waves: waves or ripples in space caused by the movement of objects in space

gravity: a force that draws objects together

neutron stars: extremely dense objects created when much larger stars collapse

plasma: a group of charged particles that is similar to gas

solar wind: a stream of charged particles flowing from the sun

sunspots: dark spots on the surface of the sun

supernovas: explosions of stars

Hamilton, John. *Hubble Space Telescope: Photographing the Universe.* Minneapolis: Abdo, 2017.

Hawksett, David. *Our Sun: Can You Figure Out Its Mysteries?* New York: PowerKids, 2018.

Morey, Allan. *The Hubble Space Telescope.* Minneapolis: Bellwether Media, 2018.

NASA: Hubblesite
http://hubblesite.org

NASA: The Sun
https://www.nasa.gov/sun

Roland, James. *Black Holes: A Space Discovery Guide.* Minneapolis: Lerner Publications, 2017.

Stars and Galaxies
https://www.esa.int/esaKIDSen/Starsandgalaxies.html

Sun Lab
http://www.pbs.org/wgbh/nova/labs/lab/sun

INDEX

Photo Acknowledgments

Image credits: NSF/LIGO/Sonoma State University/A. Simonnet, p. 4; NASA/C. Henze, p. 5; NASA, p. 6; NASA, ESA, and the Hubble Heritage Team (STScI/AURA), pp. 7, 9, 10, 12; ESA/Hubble, NASA and H. Olofsson/Onsala Space Observatory, p. 8; Stocktrek Images/Getty Images, p. 11; NASA, ESA, A. Goobar (Stockholm University), and the Hubble Heritage Team (STScI/AURA), p. 13; NASA/JPL-Caltech, pp. 14, 29; ESA/D. Ducros, p. 15; ESO, p. 16; NASA, ESA, and T. Brown (STScI), p. 17; NASA, ESA, and the Hubble SM4 ERO Team, p. 18; AdStock/Universal Images Group/Getty Images, p. 19; NASA/SDO, pp. 20, 21, 22, 24; Vincent Demers Photography/Getty Images, p. 23; ESA/J. Mai, p. 25; ESA/AEI/Milde Marketing/ Exozet (main), p. 26; ESA/EADS Astrium, p. 26 (inset); ESA, NASA, S. Beckwith (STScI) and the HUDF Team, Northrop Grumman Aerospace Systems/STScI/ATG medialab, p. 27; Bilgin S. Sasmaz/Anadolu Agency/Getty Images, p. 28. Design element: filo/DigitalVision Vectors/Getty Images.

Cover: ESA/Hubble.